The Pillow Book of

Erotica

Crown Publishers Inc.
New York

Conceived and produced by Breslich & Foss, London

Designed by Cooper Wilson Design
Origination by Dot Gradations
Printed and bound in Hong Kong

Published by Crown Publishers, Inc., 201 East 50th Street, New York,
New York 10022. Member of the Crown Publishing Group.
Random House, Inc. New York, Toronto, London, Sydney, Auckland.
CROWN is a trademark of Crown Publishers, Inc.

ISBN 0-517-59633-4

Contents

Introduction

*F*rom the eighth century Japanese poet Akahito to the ultra-modern Nicholson Baker, the pieces in THE PILLOW BOOK OF EROTICA cover a wide spectrum of sexual view-points and moods as well as styles and tones — the ache of desire, the immediacy of passion, the joy of release, and, most of all, the excitement and magic of a sexually harmonious duet between two people who understand each other's needs, and in fulfilling them, more than meet their own. The best erotic writing often comes from the most unlikely sources: that most respectable of Victorian poets, Elizabeth Barrett Browning felt the earth move in "starry turbulence," and wrote "...we felt the old earth spin... till/ If that same golden moon were overhead/ Or if beneath our feet, we did not know", or the reclusive, New England poet Emily Dickinson who wrote the vibrant poem of passionate longing, *Wild Nights*.

We hope that the writing and pictures in this book will be an inspiration to create your own erotica. There is space to record your fantasies and sensual experiences in the back of this book. If there is something you want to communicate and don't quite dare to say out loud, writing it down and leaving it lying around someplace where a lover can stumble upon it accidentally can give a whole new impetus to your sex life. Until you're inspired, why not leave this book open at Michelle Renee Pichon's inviting poem *Teach Me?*

You might discover something new.

Desire

When I say I want a man, I mean this man; if it's not that man, then it just won't do for me.

Eimi Yamada
from The X-Rated Blanket

Wild Nights—Wild Nights!
        Were I with thee
Wild Nights should be
Our luxury!

Futile—the Winds—
To a Heart in port—
Done with the Compass—
Done with the Chart!

Rowing in Eden
Ah, the Sea!
Might I but moor—Tonight—
In Thee!

Emily Dickinson
Wild Nights—Wild Nights!

When she rises in the morning
    I linger to watch her;
She spreads the bath-cloth underneath the window
And the sunbeams catch her
Glistening white on the shoulders,
While down her sides the mellow
Golden shadow glows as
She stoops to the sponge; and her swung breasts
Sway like full-blown yellow
Gloire de Dijon roses.

D.H. Lawrence
from Gloire de Dijon

Crimson nor yellow roses, nor
   The savour of the mounting sea
Are worth the perfume I adore
That clings to thee.

The languid-headed lilies tire,
The changeless waters weary me.
I ache with passionate desire
Of thine and thee.

There are but these things in the world—
Thy mouth of fire,
Thy breasts, thy hands, thy hair upcurled,
And my desire!

Theodore Wratislaw
ΕΡΟΣ Δ'ΑΥΤΕ

I wish I were close
    To you as the wet skirt of
A salt girl to her body.
I think of you always.

Akahito
Close

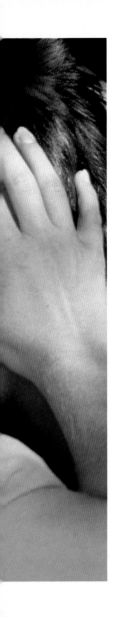

As for me, I dreamed simply of a dark-haired man bending over me to brush my lips with his burning red mouth and I woke up overwhelmed, palpitating and happier than I had ever imagined I could possibly be.

George Sand
from Lelia

Seduction

Whatever happens with us, your body
will haunt mine. . .

Adrienne Rich
from The Floating Poem, Unnumbered

i want you
to teach me
i'm ready to learn

i want you to teach me
the warmth of your breath
the weight of your body
i want to experience
the trembles heat
sweatfireiceconvulsionsgaspsthrustsspasmscaressescriesscreamsuntil. . .
    i
        can   barely
                        breathe
educate me with your
mouth tongue shoulders arms fingers
chest hips thighs legs feet toes

i want you
to teach me

i'm ready
to learn

class begins
            right

                now

Michelle Renée Pichon
from Teach Me

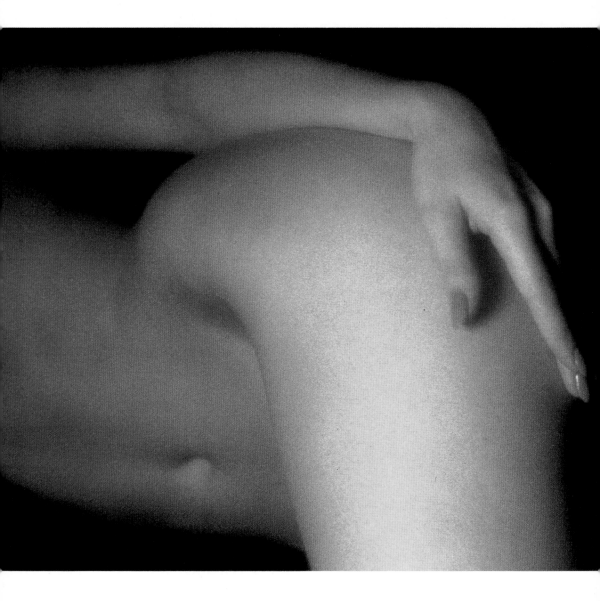

*L*ying asleep between the strokes of night
    I saw my love lean over my sad bed,
Pale as the duskiest lily's leaf or head,
Smooth skinned and dark, with bare throat made to bite,
Too wan for blushing and too warm for white,
But perfect coloured without white or red.
And her lips opened amorously, and said—
I wist not what, saving one word—Delight.
And all her face was honey to my mouth,
And all her body pasture to mine eyes;
The long lithe arms and hotter hands than fire,
The quivering flanks, hair smelling of the south,
The bright light feet, the splendid supple thighs
And glittering eyelids of my soul's desire.

Algernon Charles Swinburne
Love and Sleep

*O*h, I love moving my hands over you under your loose shirt, I love that. I'd slide my hands around over your stomach, so that my fingertips met, and feel it pull in, and slide up slowly along your ribs, and when I got to where the curves of your breasts started, I would trace them around, out to the sides, back to the middle, and I would pass just my fingertips up between your breasts, up along your breastbone, pushing under the loose bra, and then one finger even higher, along your voice box, to where your chin starts, and you'd lean your head back and I would be able to smell your hair, and then I'd pull back down, deliberately avoiding your breasts."

Nicholson Baker
from VOX

I was afraid to raise my eyelids, but looked out and saw perfectly under the lashes. The fair girl went on her knees and bent over me, fairly gloating. There was a deliberate voluptuousness which was both thrilling and repulsive, and as she arched her neck she actually licked her lips like an animal, till I could see in the moonlight the moisture shining on the scarlet lips and on the red tongue as it lapped the white sharp teeth. Lower and lower went her head as the lips went below the range of my mouth and chin and seemed about to fasten on my throat. Then she paused, and I could hear the churning sound of her tongue as it licked her teeth and lips, and could feel the hot breath on my neck. Then the skin of my throat began to tingle as one's flesh does when the hand that is to tickle it approaches nearer—nearer. I could feel the soft, shivering touch of the lips on the supersensitive skin of my throat, and the hard dents of two sharp teeth, just touching and pausing there. I closed my eyes in a languorous ecstasy and waited— waited with a beating heart.

Bram Stoker
from Dracula

*S*he broke off abruptly, and they stared at each other. "Do you know what you're saying?" Angela whispered. And Stephen answered: "I know that I love you, and that nothing else matters in the world."

Then, perhaps because of that glamorous evening, with its spirit of queer, unearthly adventure, with its urge to strange, unendurable sweetness, Angela moved a step nearer to Stephen, then another, until their hands were touching. And all that she was and all that she had been and would be again, perhaps even tomorrow, was fused at that moment into one mighty impulse, one imperative need, and that need was Stephen. Stephen's need was now hers, by sheer force of its blind and uncomprehending will to appeasement.

Then Stephen took Angela into her arms, and she kissed her full on the lips, as a lover.

Radclyffe Hall
from The Well of Loneliness

Consummation

I put my arms around him yes and drew
him down to me so he could feel my
breasts all perfume yes and his heart was
going like mad and yes I said yes I will
Yes.

James Joyce
from Ulysses

*W*here does Monsieur wish to go?" inquired the driver. "Anywhere you like!" said Léon, pushing Emma into the vehicle.

It lumbered off.

Down the rue Grand-Pont they went, crossed the place des Arts, the quai Napoléon, the Pont Neuf, and stopped short in front of the statue of Pierre Corneille.

"Drive on!" said a voice from within.

The cab set off again, and, gathering speed on the slope which leads down from the place La Fayette, swung into the station yard at a hand–gallop.

"No, straight on!" cried the same voice.

It passed through the city gates, and once on the public promenade, trotted gently between the rows of great elms. The driver mopped his forehead, put his leather hat between his legs, and, cutting across the side-walk, took a course along the river, skirting the turf. He followed the tow-path with its surface of dry pebbles, and drove on a long way towards Oyssel, beyond the islands. But suddenly he increased his speed, dashed through Quatremares, Sotteville, La Grande Chaussée and the rue d'Elbœuf, stopping for the third time in front of the Zoological Gardens.

"Get on, will you!" cried the voice more angrily than ever. Resuming its journey, the cab went by Saint-Sever, the quai des Curandiers, the quai aux Meules, crossed the bridge again into the place Champ-de-Mars, rumbling past the gardens of the hospital where old men in black coats were sunning themselves, and along a terrace green with ivy. It went back up the boulevard Bouvreuil, on along the boulevard Cauchoise, and up Mont-Riboudet and so to the hill of Deville.

There it turned, and aimlessly, without taking any definite direction, drove on at random. . .

Occasionally he attempted to draw up, only to hear behind him exclamations of fury. Then he lashed more vigorously than ever at his sweating jades; heedless of jolts he pursued his career, bumping into various obstacles, but not caring; demoralized and almost in tears from thirst, fatigue and misery.

Down at the harbour, in a hurly-burly of wagons and casks, along the streets, at various milestones, the citizens stared wide-eyed at that most extraordinary of all sights in a provincial town—a carriage with drawn blinds, constantly reappearing, more secret than a tomb and bucketing like a ship at sea . . .

At last, about six o'clock, the cab stopped in a lane of the Beauvoisine quarter, and a woman got out. She walked away with her veil lowered, and did not once turn her head.

Gustave Flaubert
from Madame Bovary

*T*he moth's kiss first!
    Kiss me as if you made believe
You were not sure, this eve,
How my face, your flower, had pursed
Its petals up; so, here and there
You brush it, till I grow aware
Who wants me, and wide ope I burst.

The bee's kiss, now!
Kiss me as if you entered gay
My heart at some noonday,
A bud that dares not disallow
The claim, so all is rendered up,
And passively its shattered cup
Over your head to sleep I bow.

Robert Browning
from In a Gondola

I flung closer to his breast,
　　As sword that, after battle, flings to sheathe;
And, in that hurtle of united souls,
The mystic motions which in common moods
Are shut beyond our sense, broke in on us,
And, as we sate, we felt the old earth spin,
And all the starry turbulence of worlds
Swing round us in their audient circles, till
If that same golden moon were overhead
Or if beneath our feet, we did not know.

Elizabeth Barrett Browning
from Aurora Leigh

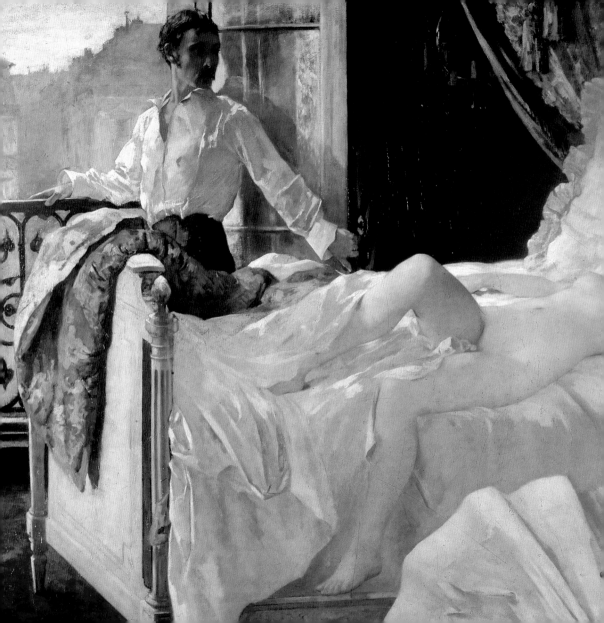

Afterglow

The room, which was dimly lit by a
lamp, was slumbering in the warm, damp
odour of love. . . There was a sigh; then
a kiss broke the silence. . .

Emile Zola
from Nana

When I go away from you
          The world beats dead
Like a slackened drum.
I call out for you against the jutted stars
And shout into the ridges of the wind.
Streets coming fast,
One after the other,
Wedge you away from me,
And the lamps of the city prick my eyes
So that I can no longer see your face.
Why should I leave you,
To wound myself upon the sharp
          edges of the night?

Amy Lowell
The Taxi

He slept with her right breast cupped in his left hand, for she had her back to him. And she knew that at first he must have slept with his wife like that, because his hand came like a child's, and gathered her breast and held it as in a cup. If she moved his hand it came back while he slept, by instinct, and found her breast and held it softly enclosed. And it was as if he balanced the whole of her gently in the hollow of his hand, as if she were no more than a dove nestling, all nestled in the strong palm of his hand.

She lay perfectly still, yet not asleep. All her body was asleep under the heavy arm laid across her. Only her mind, like a small star of consciousness, shone faintly and wondered. His arm lay across her, her breast was balanced in his hand, she was encircled and enclosed by him even while he slept.

D.H. Lawrence
from The First Lady Chatterley

*S*ome day, when I lose you,
    will you be able to sleep without
my whispering myself away
like a linden's crown above you?

Without my waking here and laying down
words, almost like eyelids,
upon your breasts, upon your limbs,
upon your mouth?

Without my closing you and leaving
you alone with what is yours,
like a garden with a mass
of melissas and star–anise?

Rainer Maria Rilke
Slumbersong

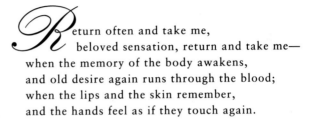

*R*eturn often and take me,
 beloved sensation, return and take me—
when the memory of the body awakens,
and old desire again runs through the blood;
when the lips and the skin remember,
and the hands feel as if they touch again.

Return often and take
me at night, when the
lips and the skin
remember . . .

C. P. Cavafy
Return

What lips my lips have kissed, and where, and why,
  I have forgotten, and what arms have lain
Under my head till morning; but the rain
Is full of ghosts tonight, that tap and sigh
Upon the glass and listen for reply,
And in my heart there sits a quiet pain
For unremembered lads that not again
Will turn to me at midnight with a cry.
Thus in the winter stands the lonely tree,
Nor knows what birds have vanished one by one,
Yet knows its boughs more silent than before:
I cannot say what loves have come and gone,
I only know that summer sang in me
A little while, that in me sings no more.

Edna St. Vincent Millay
Sonnet

Reflections

My Own Erotica

Some people like sex more than others—
You seem to like it a lot.
There's nothing wrong with being
innocent or high–minded,
But I'm glad you're not.

Wendy Cope
Some People

Acknowledgments

p.9 The extract from "The X-Rated Blanket" by Eimi Yamada from NEW JAPANESE VOICES edited by Helen Mitsios, Copyright © 1991 by Helen Mitsios. Used with the permission of Grove/Atlantic Monthly Press.

p.27 The extract from "VOX" by Nicholson Baker, Copyright © 1992 Nicholson Baker, is reprinted by kind permission of Random House, Inc.

p.34-5 The extract from from Madame Bovary by Gustave Flaubert, translated by Gerard Hopkins, Oxford University Press, reprinted by permission of Oxford University Press.

p.45 The extract from The First Lady Chatterley by D.H. Lawrence reprinted by permission of Laurence Pollinger Ltd. and the Estate of Frieda Lawrence Ravagli.

p. 51 "What Lips My Lips have Kissed" by Edna St. Vincent Millay. From COLLECTED POEMS, HarperCollins. Copyright © 1921, 1948 by Edna St. Vincent Millay. Reprinted by permission of Elizabeth Barnett, literary executor.

p.53 "Some People" by Wendy Cope. From MAKING COCOA FOR KINGSLEY AMIS, Faber & Faber Ltd. Reprinted by permission of Faber & Faber Ltd.

Every effort has been made to trace the copyright holders of the quoted material. If, however, there are any omissions, these can be rectified in any future editions.

© Bridgeman Art Library, *pp.3, 8, 34, 36, 40, 44*; © Steve Curd, *p.48*; © Peter G. Dobson/ Amber Visual, *p.12*; © Fine Art Photographs, *p.50*; © Mike Henton, pp.20, 26, 42; Image Bank © Werner Bokelberg *p.14*, Yuri Dojc *p.22, 30*, Robert Farber, *p.24, 28*, Don Allen Sparks, *p.46*; © Leo Lyons, *p.18*; © Private Collection, Switzerland, Photo: Christian Poite, *p.38*; © Zefa, *pp.10, 16, 32*

Additional photography by Nigel Bradley and Jacqui Hurst